34134 00238974 7

Leabhar...

KU-071-306

RESOURCE CENTRE
This book belongs to:

Bragar

Published by Ladybird Books Ltd
A Penguin Company
Penguin Books Ltd, 80 Strand, London WC2R 0RL, UK
Penguin Books Australia Ltd, Camberwell, Victoria, Australia
Penguin Books (NZ) Ltd, Cnr Airbourne and Rosedale Roads, Albany, Auckland, 1310, New Zealand

1 3 5 7 9 10 8 6 4 2

© LADYBIRD BOOKS MMV

LADYBIRD and the device of a Ladybird are trademarks of Ladybird Books Ltd
All rights reserved. No part of this publication may be reproduced,
stored in a retrieval system, or transmitted in any form or by any means,
electronic, mechanical, photocopying, recording or otherwise,
without the prior consent of the copyright owner.

Printed in Italy

Pirates

written by Lorraine Horsley
illustrated by Martin Hargreaves

Here are some famous
pirates.

Bartholomew
Portugues

Sir Henry
Morgan

Anne Bonny

Blackbeard

When pirates were at sea,
they sailed in big ships
like this.

Jolly Roger
flag

cannon

sail

9

When pirates were at sea,
they ate food like this.

grog (rum
and water)

dried
meat

hard tack
(dry biscuit)

turtle
eggs

11

When pirates were at sea,
they wore clothes like this.

canvas trousers
made from sails

woollen shirt
waterproofed
with tar

When pirates were at sea,
they did jobs like this.

mending
rope

scrubbing
the deck

mending
sails

cleaning
weapons

When pirates were at sea,
they had fun like this.

playing
cards

dancing

When pirates were at sea, they fought with weapons like this.

cutlass

When pirates were at sea, they attacked other ships like this.

Some pirates took treasure like this.

jewels

gold

silk

charts

23

Some pirates hid treasure like this.

When pirates were at sea,
they said things like this.

Ahoy there me hearties!

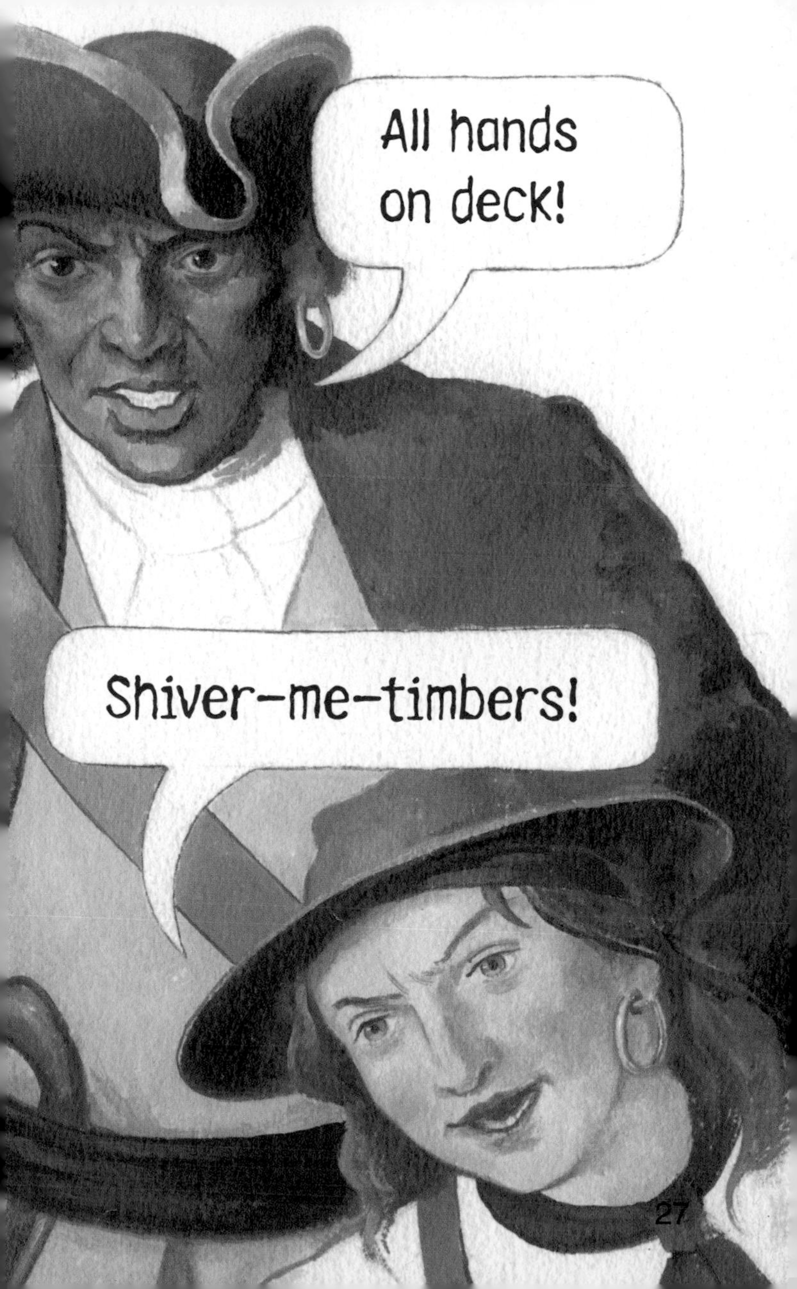
All hands on deck!
Shiver-me-timbers!

What would you do if you were a pirate?

sail big ships

eat pirate food

steal treasure

dance

Index